My Pet Map

By Cameron Macintosh

It is my pet map.

I can see Tim and his pet.

His pet is Nat the rat.

Pen has a pet cat.

Bab is her pet cat.

Fin is **my** pet.

Fin taps at the pet map!

The pet map can fit Fin!

Tap, tap, tap!

Fin pats the pet map!

Pat, pat, pat!

CHECKING FOR MEANING

1. What are the names of the pets mentioned in the story? *(Literal)*

2. What does Fin do to the pet map? *(Literal)*

3. Why do you think Fin wants to be on the pet map? *(Inferential)*

EXTENDING VOCABULARY

pet	Look at the word *pet*. Can you think of other words that rhyme with *pet*?
fit	Look at the word *fit*. What does *fit* mean in the story?
tap	Look at the word *tap*. Can you think of other words that mean the same as *tap*?

MOVING BEYOND THE TEXT

1. Why do you think Fin's owner is making a pet map?

2. How might the story be different if Fin couldn't fit on the pet map?

3. Can you think of other ways the pets in the story could interact with the pet map?

4. What other animals might be part of a pet map?

SPEED SOUNDS

Cc	Bb	Rr	Ee	Ff	Hh	Nn

Mm	Ss	Aa	Pp	Ii	Tt

PRACTICE WORDS

can

pet

Nat

rat

Pen

cat

Bab

fit

Fin